An Autopsy

Hunter Bloodmoon

An Autopsy

Hunter Bloodmoon

This work CC-BY-NC-SA Hunter Bloodmoon 2025
ISBN (print): 978-19-15952-36-3
ISBN (digital): 978-19-15952-37-0

First published 21 January, 2025 by Sphinx/Sul Books

Cover Design: RITONA & Hunter Bloodmoon
Image Credit: Xavier Lopez
Interior design and editing: RITONA

Sphinx and RITONA are sister imprints of
Sul Books, LTD

See our other titles at SULBOOKS.COM

Within

Introduction — 7
Wishing Well — 9
Silt Mouth — 10
Tundra — 12
Watusi — 13
All Hail the Runners — 15
Say My Name — 17
Yellow Tape & White Carpet — 18
Veil — 21
Surrender — 23
A Treatise on Crazy — 25
Save Me — 27
Tenderize — 28
Ribcage — 29
What Happened on the Way to the Ocean — 31
debris — 32
Calculations — 33
Broken — 34
don't pick up hitch hikers — 36
skitter — 37
gape — 38
marathon — 39
spin spin spin — 40
forest — 41
to whom it may concern — 42
naval — 43
The Kettle & The Hearth — 44
untitled — 45
Din — 46
Devil's Pool — 48
Dedication — 50
About — 51

DROP TOW AND GO

WILLIAM ASA SWAN IV

MAY 7, 1958 ~ FEBRUARY 3, 2019

Introduction

There's a strange and wild and dangerous truth I found because of Hunter's poems. Often when you find your own voice, others find theirs, too. Often when you liberate yourself, others get the same idea.

It shouldn't seem so strange, really. I mean, this is technically how revolutions have always started. Someone gets tired of licking boots all the time, and finally decides to stop. Then, another person, who really never liked the taste of boots but was just pretending they did, decides that maybe they don't have to lick them anymore, either. And then next thing you know, there's a lot of people not licking boots anymore, and the ones whose boots were being licked suddenly have to learn to clean their boots on their own.

What I really mean is that Hunter's poems are spells of contagious self-reclamation, the kind that comes from being really damn honest with yourself. Yeah, that kind of honesty can taste bitter, especially when you have to be brutally honest about flaws and sadness and especially about your pain.

But — boots don't really taste good. Sure, we might say we like the way they taste, or that we don't really mind, but we're not really being very honest with ourselves, are we? And then, when we start to be a bit honest about things, suddenly there's this bitter and generally unpleasant taste in our mouth, and we make the mistake of thinking that's what honesty tastes like. But really, that's just the taste of the boots we've been licking, and honesty is telling us that we don't really like licking them at all.

Still not convinced? That's okay. Go read my favorite poem in this collection, All Hail The Runners. When I read it, the first few lines tasted really, really bitter:

I used to believe that
the greatest act of love
was to sacrifice
to be supple
to bend like a bridge

They all tasted really bitter because that was, at the time I read the poem, exactly what I still believed. Sure, I would have told you instead that I was sacrificing myself for "just a little while" until the abusive man whose boots I was licking realized he was being abusive. (Well, actually, I had lots of other explanations, but they were all various and really dishonest versions of "I like the taste of boots.")

Reading that poem made me be honest with myself. Sure, it tasted really damn bitter, but that wasn't Hunter's fault, and that wasn't the taste of honesty, either. It was just the taste of the boots I didn't want to lick anymore, and so I decided to stop licking them.

Hunter has written lots of other poems with this same magic, and I'm pretty excited you're going to get to read them. And if you notice sometimes a bitter taste in your mouth, you're probably about to learn something really strange and wild and powerful about yourself, too.

—Rhyd Wildermuth

Wishing Well

I am at the bottom of a well
and the well's name is
horror.

I am buried under the sand of a giant desert
and the desert's name is loss.

I am in the belly of the storm,
no eye in sight,
and the storm's name is regret.

Silt Mouth

I dream of fire,
but
lately,
my dreams
are an ocean with no end.
Mind dragging the bottom,
sucking on silt.
Lost in the tangles
of mermaid hair and trident spears.

I want to sink,
one last time,
into the arms of my memory of you
and try to taste
what it was that I loved about you.
I want to bury my face
into the hollow of your neck and shoulder
the space that my
heart fit so well
and release
ululating cries and seas of unshed
mourning.

Come here, my love.
Let me remember you.

While I wait
to be swept away,
mute and stricken.
Trying to plug leaks in a dam that is collapsing
under the weight

of screams drowned before they could escape
my clenched teeth
my tightened fists.
White knuckling my
lack of control.

I now dream of waves
eroding my hopes
like mountains,
slowly,
with every
crash of the surf.

I want the fire back
I want to want again

Tundra

I had a dream
I was struggling through the snow
with biting wind scouring my cheeks.

I was trying to
get to the fire
trying to
get to the light.

I tripped
and sunk beneath
the snow banks.

Will you find me in the spring?
When all of the snow has melted
and the smell of early flowers
laces the air?
Will you have noticed that I never made it to
the fire?
That I never found
the light?

Watusi

I sail by passive
and go straight to aggressive
my polite clap

more chilling than
any war horn
at dawn

Picture this:
my blood smeared face
smiling at the wreckage
the carnage
my dancing feet
twirling
over the broken ground
no dance sweeter than
the watusi

My humor is a lash
and if it does not draw blood
it is not funny.
I am my own favorite
punchline.
Please, admire my flair.
It is the brightest flower in my bonnet

Do not try to placate me
I am not the moral
of the story
I am the foreboding clouds
the ominous roll of thunder

the ssnk ssnk of the scythe
felling the wheat
the held breath
before the arrow flies
I awaken
to crush dreams
and burn down villages.

Picture this:
A smile so sharp
it can draw blood
a flash of
anger is all it takes
to light my
finest summer bonnet
aflame.

Run.

All Hail the Runners

I used to believe that
the greatest act of love
was to sacrifice
to be supple
to bend like a bridge
to let you in
like I was inviting you to
tea
cake
everything

Now that I am older
I understand that this is just
a lie told to young girls
by men of your ilk
to consume
possess and conquer
young girls,
Turning them into old girls
and then throwing them away-
If they do not run first

I ran.
I ran so fast
my lips blistered and my skin cracked
while your howls followed me
for years and years
proclaiming your love hate and ownership of me
attempting to reassert your control,
to claim your land.

My body is not acreage
and
I am not what you failed to make me.
Promises made while the beast is hidden
Do Not Count
when locked in a tower
dressed in rags,
and it took at least a quarter
to relearn to trust my voice

That is the hardest part.
I forgot I had a voice,
because whenever I opened my mouth
your voice
came out

Do not listen to the pretty lies
that fall out of the lips
of those who wish
to hold your fire
only to put it out.

All hail the runners

Say My Name

My heart is a whore.
Let me spread
my ventricles,
like my legs,
wide and open.

An autopsy with
too many names on it.

Reaching out
for you with my
pulmonary veins,
like grasping,
seeking hands.

Take you deep
into my
vena cava
and never
ever
let you go.

An autopsy with
too many names on it.

Yellow Tape & White Carpet

I grew up haunted
unwanted
except by
the bog lady
leading me to her special
spot for the best cranberries.

Come, little girl…
I have a secret to tell you.

(crawling under the beams
cheek pressed tight to the dirt
clawing cobwebs from
my eyes
I realize that
I am my own bar with
KEEP OUT
DON'T EVER GO THAT FAR
written on it.)

I grew up possessed
distressed
swallowed by memories
dipped in head first.
My mind is a cup
that is overflowing
sploshing all over
the fancy white carpet.

(And Lo! An angel
appeared
and whispered
secrets that I have forgotten)

I sleep
and dream
of unrelenting glimpses
of happiness.

(memories slip up
like gas trapped in a tar pit
telling me all those secrets
again and again.
always too late to prevent
the slackjawed
train wreck I create)

I grew up haunted.
Unwanted.
I dream that that will change
that I will be seen.
Heard.
I grew up, but not out,
trapped in that
bog or tar pit
only glimpsed
in nightmares
and torn fragments
of hazy memories.

*(look at me,
come on,
see me.)*

It will never be me,
for I spilled my
heart's blood all over
your fancy white carpet.
and I have no more
to give.

Veil

I thought about it,
just so you know.
And I took the steps
right in front of me,

leading away from you.
Maybe this was not your
desired result, my panicked flight,
But too bad,
done is done
as they say.

I am trying to figure out
what really went wrong.

You said you liked my hair long,
and I admit, I liked you pulling it.
So, the only natural thing to do
was to cut it off.
I did leave some long for you,
so you could have a reminder
of your own happy picture.
But the day has arrived
and this white dress doesn't hug my hips.
my hands are itching in these gloves,
and these shoes, they do not fit.
I cannot see through the lace
and I am falling down,
tripping over this train
that I missed
because I could not run fast enough.

Full frantic flight cut short
by my own need for closure.
Turning slowly I stood my ground
as you pulled it out beneath me.
Like I was no more than a table cloth,
needing to be swept away and cleaned.
And watching as I said the words I never wanted to say,
spilling out of my mouth:
"I love you, too."
See, you caught me by surprise.
Off guard.
A startled fawn,
rushing to kiss your car.
And does any of this really matter?
Besides the fact that I am kicking
myself for falling
over,
and wanting nothing more
than to be held
in your high regard?

Surrender

There is a wild creature that lives inside me.

We used to be one,
but in an effort to please,
placate,
soothe,
I ripped her from me
piece by piece.
every claw, every tooth.
I caged her —
thinking that maybe if I tame myself
I will be good enough,
no longer too much,
too wild.
Untamed.
Untamable.

She stalks the confines
of my heart,
teeth gnashing
tail lashing
and prowls the borders of my mind —
muzzle twitching
hackles undulating, like the sea.
She snarls at me from her prison.
She howls at me
to let her out —
to become one
like we are meant to be.
In her cage she paces.
Starving.

I am scared to release her,
after all I did to sever her from me,
will the pieces of her
fit back
into the wounds
I created
when I tore myself
apart?

Will I ever be able to forgive myself
for the lengths I took
to unmake the very thing
that made me who I am?

A Treatise on Crazy

I feel the loneliness
bubble under my skin
like blisters
the teeny tiny ones I get
during an eczema flare,
it itches my brain
and makes me say things
I regret
and I hate when my brain gets crazy.
Crazy. That's a funny word
so loaded,
like the potatoes I made last week.
Maybe I'm dying,
left to rot as a
housewife
in a forgotten kitchen.
Is that why I'm lonely?
The kettle is whistling.
Where was I?
Oh yes. In the kitchen,
at the stove.
Blisters bubbling
like boiling water.
My lover, he says he understands
but I don't think
he does.
The kettle is whistling
and I leave it
to cover up the sounds of my tears
the crazy is
bubbling under my skin

like blisters
I took my heels off —
just for a minute
and pretended that my toes
were curling in the sand
on some tropical beach.
Why is the waiter telling me the
kettle is boiling?
Can't a lady get some peace
for just a second?
A second!
May I please have a second of your time?
The roof needs repair
the children need to see the dentist
No!
My teeth are not on edge
and my jaw is not clenched
Yes, I do look tired
I shall go powder my nose,
hoping to
smooth out the fine lines
with so many tinctures and creams

My loneliness is
bubbling under my skin
like blisters.
I forgot to use a pot holder again.

Save Me

I am drowning.
All of the clocks
in this house
are wrong
and I am drowning.
Ticking seconds
are the waves
shoving me under.

I am drowning.

Tenderize

Could you make my memories
soft again?
Warm and tender
to the touch
Instead of a box
of razor blades.

Ribcage

I will never grow tired of rattling cages
It does not matter if it is mine or yours
I love to hear the clanking of the bars
The rattling of bones
The shrieks in the night
Of my fears dying, one by one

Did you know that I have the key?
There is an escape
And there is a way out
Don't follow the light,
It is not for you and I.

I follow the scent on the wind
The promise of winter's crisp breath
I follow the sound of a branch breaking
Nock Draw Anchor Aim
Release.
A breath for the taking

I will never grow tired of
Shedding skin
Whether it is mine or yours
It matters not when we are becoming
Other, becoming whole under the open sky

Did you know that I care not
For the opinions of your gate keepers?
I only ask
To drive this nail home
that I have no masters

and this cage is only kept around
for the rattling
a score for the settling
bones for the breaking

Like a snake
I flick flick flick
my lids and silvery tongue
while cities fall to dust
and my doubts slide
like a slip off my unbent
unbroken back.
Attend!
Watch closely
As I destroy any bonds
Placed upon me
Time and time again
With a ululating cry
To battle

What Happened on the Way to the Ocean

One day I will be whole
but not today

I will rip my faithless heart
from my chest
and place it on the block
sold to the lowest bidder

I will tear this lying tongue out
to the root
from my mouth
and throw it in the fire
to spark and splutter

One day my mind
will not be an open wound
but not today

I will carve out my tar stained soul
by the teeth
and throw it in the ocean
to drown
with the mermaids

DEBRIS

need to remember
to relearn how to breathe.
to fold the towels.
to stop the
skittering
of my fingers across my skin
searching .... searching.
let me rip open my
imperfections
for your amusement.
searching .... searching.
can I scour the
traces of my
insecurity from my skin?
need to remember
to relearn how to exhale.
to wash the dishes.
scrape
all of me into the trash
with the scraps from
dinner
as I disappear into
the carpet.

Calculations

"How long does it take to disappear?" I whisper
as I trace my face with my always moving
shifting
calculating
eyes

Does it happen all at once
or does it take x amount
of times of not being noticed?

Broken

I am aware that I am unkind.
It does not matter,
there is no heart in here to reach.
Like a wave, I cannot help
but to slam against the cliffs,
as if I am asking
if erosion
can return a heart that is missing?

I feel like a hearth
without a home.
A pilgrimage without
a destination.
Reverence
without a reason.
How do I feel so
full
while starving?

I am aware that I am not so much as lost
as just refusing to go the right way.
The first time I realized this
I cried tears of hot rage
at the rivers edge
alone, as always.
Clothed only in
molten tears and frigid dreams.
How do I always end up here?
Like a fever, I cannot help
but breaking in the end.

I feel like a
secret
without a source.
A destination
that no one visits.
A shrine that
no one remembers.
How do I feel so
full
while starving?

I am aware that I am a sea
without a shore.
Like a wave, I cannot help
but spill across the floor,
in sheets,
like a shroud.
Or an excuse.

Like a fever, I cannot help
but breaking in the end.
It is only the beginning,
and I hear that
once broken,
a new heart can grow
from the wasteland.

DON'T PICK UP HITCH HIKERS

Snow covers the ground
there is a certain kind of silence
that follows
A hush that smothers
any attempt at sound
Except for the rage in
my head and
my heart

I burn too hot
too hard
for this kind of silence
just tell me
anything
Everything

SKITTER

today my brain is restless
pacing like a panther
in a too small cage
rustling the papers
that have accumulated
in piles
shoved into the back
corners of my brain

today my brain is protesting
the weight of
too many thoughts
too many problems
with no solutions

GAPE

I sent the last letter
into the abyss today
who knows if that gaping maw
will tender a reply

I suppose the better question is why I bothered

MARATHON

something stirs
just under the surface
I can see it
undulating
I can see it
shifting

and here I am
6 under
and I still cannot think of anything other than you
code and syntax cannot distract me
from how much
and how deeply
my love for you runs
and let me tell you
I know how to
fucking run

SPIN SPIN SPIN

and when I spiral out
like a dervish
where is my safety net?

is it a tattered sail
a rotten cloth?
it does not seem to matter
what I say
so it should not matter
when I give reassurance
that I am not demanding your time

and when I cry
like a waterfall
will you learn how to swim?

FOREST

I don't know why
I always come back here
back to this
never healing
wound

even the happy things
remind me that
I am sad
alone
with nothing to give
nothing to gain

should just
tuck my tail between my legs
and go out into the forest
to die

TO WHOM IT MAY CONCERN

dear father
will anyone tell me
when you die?
just like you
could never
tell me that
you love me
while you live?
or even,
heaven forfend,
that you have
ever been proud of me?
that I have ever been
more than a blip
on your radar?
or an annoyance in
court
for child support?
the little girl inside
of me
breaks
over the wanting
the needing
of any scrap
any pittance
of your affection.
dear father
will I need to care
when you die?

NAVAL

I am in the belly
of a monster
called despair
can't help
but always end up back here
despite best,
or any,
intentions.
it always ends
with me
face down
choking on the acids
as despair
digests me.

The Kettle & The Hearth

Tea Time:

> I could drink green curry
> like water from your lips,
> awash in a verdant haze.
> Longing to never wake-
> to never surrender this
> Becoming-Bliss.
> My will has dissolved into
> the finest soma
> and all my dreams becoming
> the favored liqueur of the Gods.

The Ashes:

> I spoon jam sparingly
> onto a piece of toast
> hoping to add moisture
> to this texture of cardboard.
> All I know is that if this
> famine does not end soon
> there will be nothing left
> except a spoon, an empty jar of jam
> and a sheet of cardboard.

UNTITLED

When I was small I wanted
to be a pirate ship.

DIN

This silence is deafening —
like the roaring of the ocean from

a broken seashell —
cracked open during a raging storm
that I unleashed like a pack of rabid hounds
in order to clear the air of the scent of you,
but the memory is not so easily erased
because the only sound ringing in my ears
is like a prayer,
drummed loud and clear:
"No, I never did love you."

I still remember how you
are like the day I was at
the beach when I was six.
When I tried to cup the sea in my hands
to watch the waves up close,
but the sea wouldn't stay in my hands.

This silence is maddening
torn apart like my Sunday dress.
Covered in mud, delicate chiffon ripped with
only a broken seashell to
remind me of the prayer I swore I had forgotten.
I don't forget so easily — even
with the scent of southern wood on the air.
With only one final phrase
to council my decent into the
curve of a broken seashell;
where I swear I can hear the ocean.

No constancy in my dreams, no matter the incantation.
I'm far too gone to remind myself that
none of this matters
and my heart constricts in another
attempt of Heart Attack.
I just can't believe that this is all there is,
that this is what it's all come down to.
Rabid Hounds and Poppies Seashells
and broken teeth.
Where the only sound ringing in my ears
echoes like a curse bubbling up from an ocean covered
volcano,
lava hot words spewing along the surface,
pouring along the divides of our tectonic plates.

We are making mountains, you and I.
With prayers of
"No I never did love you."

Even here, even now, after all of this
has been said and done,
I still cannot wake up.
Our earthquake has found me
chasing 60 stories down in a graceful arch,
as I ride my death like
a wave cupped in my hands,
with my mouth forming the words of my prayer
to banish the memory
of how I hurt you with six simple words.

Devil's Pool

I have climbed your vertebrae,
like I have scaled Mount Everest.
While your ribcage has posed an eternal problem,
because my arms are not long enough
to grasp the spaces in between,
so I can climb you like a ladder,
to speak to you in beat — in your ear,
not quite pantomime,
but close enough to improperly reflect
gesture to gesture.
To bring you closer— to bring you near.
I need you to know how I feel —
flesh to flesh.

I seem to lick/like your skin
that place just under your chin.
Treating you like a pomegranate stained plate,
pretending to be Persephone,
stuck in a dirty kitchen,
with nothing left to cook save damned souls.

My flesh remembers the curve of you,
like fossils pressed in sand stone,
a mere impression that I long to resurrect.
To understand how my skin
craves the taste of that place,
where the blood flows thick and rich,
where I fell like Victoria Falls
from the heights of Mount Vesuvius,
when the lava flew down the slopes,
all in an effort to erase my memories of you.

Climb you, to be with you
along the crater of Halemaumau,
just like we did so long ago.
When we could look each other in the eyes without creating earthquakes
with verbal tectonic plates.
I miss the times I treated your eyes like Lake Baikal,
when all I could ponder was 'where is the end to my wonder in you?',
and if you would really let me drown.
But, I suppose my only available resource now is your
V E R T E B R A E.
Alone with the echoing reminder that your skin tastes of pomegranates,
and now that I am forced a step back,
your ribcage is not as daunting as I thought.

I must remind myself how you are like the tectonic plates sticking out above the dirt.

Dedication

I held you
and we cried
great floods of tears
rolling down our cheeks like glaciers
melting
rushing to the sea

We do not want it to rise
but rise it must.
Arms as strong as mountains
lifting me time and time again
can I touch the sky yet?
I held you
and we wept
leaving behind the ghosts
welcoming
the spectre of tomorrow.

My friend,
may you drink deep
of the joys and sorrows

About the Author

Hunter Bloodmoon lurks somewhere in the Salish Sea, plotting revolution while baking for her children.

Find her at:
WWW.HUNTERBLOODMOON.COM

About the Publisher

.Sphinx and RITONA are sister imprints of Sul Books. Born from a collaboration of two long-time independent esoteric publishers, and named to honor the Suleviae — the sisterhood of goddesses revered at springs throughout Europe — Sul Books is dedicated to publishing works that manifest aspects of the sacred sight that heals what humans have harmed

Find out more at SULBOOKS.COM.

www.ingramcontent.com/pod-product-compliance
Lightning Source LLC
Chambersburg PA
CBHW050209130526
44590CB00043B/3357